D1443686

Miraculous Magic Tricks

TABLE MAGIC

by Thomas Canavan
Illustrations by David Mostyn

WINDMILL BOOKS

New York

Published in 2014 by Windmill Books, an Imprint of Rosen Publishing
29 East 21st Street, New York, NY 10010

Copyright © 2014 by Arcturus Publishing Ltd.

First Edition

Author: Thomas Canavan
Editors: Patience Coster and Joe Harris
US Editor: Joshua Shadowens
Illustrations: David Mostyn
Design: Emma Randall

Library of Congress Cataloging-in-Publication Data

Canavan, Thomas, 1956–
Table magic / by Thomas Canavan.
    pages cm.— (Miraculous magic tricks)
Includes index.
ISBN 978-1-4777-9053-3 (library) — ISBN 978-1-4777-9054-0 (pbk.) —
ISBN 978-1-4777-9055-7 (6-pack)
1. Magic tricks—Juvenile literature. I. Title.
GV1548.C26 2014
793.8—dc23
                                2013021317

Printed in the USA

CPSIA Compliance Information: Batch # BW14WM: For further information contact Windmill Books, New York, New York at 1-866-478-0556
SL003844US

CONTENTS

INTRODUCTION

Within these pages you will discover great magic tricks that are easy to do and impressive to watch.

To be a successful magician, you will need to practice the tricks in private before you perform them in front of an audience. An excellent way to practice is in front of a mirror, since you can watch the magic happen before your own eyes.

When performing, you must speak clearly, slowly, and loudly enough for everyone to hear. But never tell the audience what's going to happen.

Remember to "watch your angles." This means being careful about where your spectators are standing or sitting when you are performing. The best place is directly in front of you.

Never tell the secret of how the trick is done. If someone asks, just say: "It's magic!"

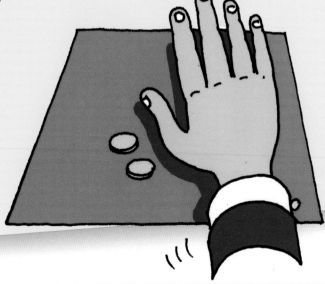

THE MAGICIAN'S PLEDGE

I promise not to reveal the secrets of magic to those who are not magicians.

I promise to practice these magic tricks over and over again before attempting to perform them in front of an audience.

I promise to respect my art, the art of magic.

THE RISING PEN

ILLUSION

The magician casts a spell over a ballpoint pen. At his command, the pen rises through his clenched fist.

1 Prior to the trick, the magician finds a small, thin elastic band and a pen with a tight, hooked clip. He loops the elastic band around his right index finger.

2 To perform the trick, the magician holds up the pen with his left hand and tells the audience he is going to cast a spell over it. He hands it round so that they can see it is not a trick pen.

3 The magician stares hard at the pen in his left hand and says: "Prepare to move." He slowly puts his right hand around his left, making sure to keep the elastic band hidden from the audience.

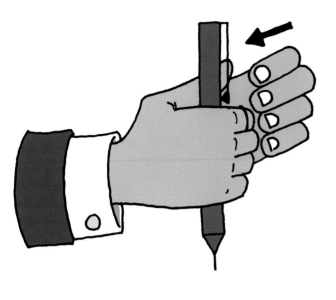

4 He slides the pen, writing point down, into his clenched right hand so that the clip catches the elastic band. Then he distracts the audience with some hand rolling.

5 During this rolling, he lets the pen flip so that the writing point faces up. The pen is still in his cupped right hand, looped onto the elastic band.

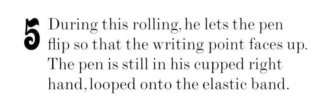

6 The magician continues muttering spells and moving his hands while secretly pulling the pen down so that the elastic stretches.

7 He stops moving his hands and says the spell is cast. He holds the pen tight with his right hand and removes his left hand with a flourish.

8 The magician now commands the pen to rise slowly. He allows it to do this by releasing his grip gradually. The elastic band will slowly pull it up. If he releases his grip more quickly, the pen will spring up in his hand.

MAGIC TIP!
FOR THIS TRICK, USE A PEN WITH A VERY TIGHT CLIP.

WHICH TOY DID YOU CHOOSE?

1 This trick depends on two things—a good number of spectators and a partner who's in on the trick.

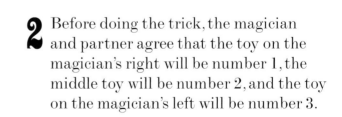

2 Before doing the trick, the magician and partner agree that the toy on the magician's right will be number 1, the middle toy will be number 2, and the toy on the magician's left will be number 3.

3 The magician turns his back to the toys and a volunteer points at one of them. The other spectators note which toy it is (one of those spectators is the magician's secret partner).

4 The magician turns and concentrates on the three toys. He moves closer and smells them and listens to them— to make it seem as though he's picking up secret information.

5 He looks into the distance while he concentrates even harder. He makes sure he can see his partner, who blinks or winks once, twice, or three times to signal which toy was chosen (number 1, 2, or 3).

6 The magician looks once more at the toys and then points to the one that was signaled by his partner.

COUNTING CONFUSION

1 The magician places three coins of the same value on the table. He says he will use them to keep track of his counting.

ILLUSION

The magician places three identical coins on the table and uses them to keep track as he counts to ten. Then he asks a spectator to do the same—but it always comes out wrong!

ONE...

2 He picks them up one by one, counting "one," "two," and "three."

SIX

3 Then he lays them out again, counting them "four," "five," and "six."

4 Saying "seven," the magician picks up one coin. Then he touches the other two, calling them "eight" and "nine."

5 He places the coin from his hand back on the table, calling it "ten."

6 The magician gathers the coins up and hands them to a spectator. He asks the spectator to repeat this simple counting. But she cannot get the trick to work, no matter how hard she tries!

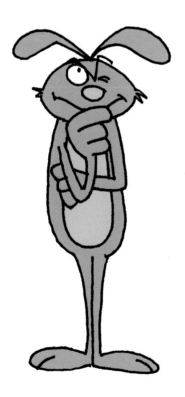

MAGIC TIP
THE SPECTATOR WILL ALMOST CERTAINLY BEGIN COUNTING WHILE PUTTING THE COINS DOWN, AND NOT WHILE PICKING THEM UP. THAT MAKES IT IMPOSSIBLE TO GET THE TRICK TO WORK!

PEPPER CHASE

ILLUSION

A volunteer is invited to stick a finger into a bowl of water with pepper floating on the surface. Nothing happens. When the water is calm again, the magician does the same thing and the pepper scoots away from his finger.

1 Prior to the trick, the magician squeezes some dishwashing liquid onto his index finger.

2 To perform the trick, the magician pours water into a shallow soup bowl until it is nearly full.

3 He sprinkles or grinds pepper over the water until the surface is almost covered.

4 The magician then asks a volunteer to dip his finger into the water. Nothing much happens.

5 The magician waits for the water to become calm again. Then he dips his index finger into the water.

6 The pepper zooms away from his finger to the edge of the bowl.

MAGIC ICE HOIST

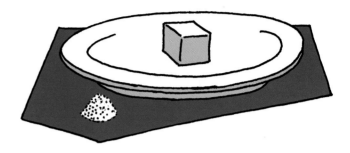

ILLUSION

The magician lays a piece of string on top of an ice cube and concentrates for a while. Then he holds each end of the string and lifts—and the ice cube sticks to the string.

1 The magician places an ice cube in the middle of a dinner plate. Beneath the lip of the plate—on the side that is out of view of the audience—is a small pile of table salt about the size of a small grape.

MAGIC TIP!
THIS TRICK DEPENDS ON USING ONE HAND TO DISTRACT ATTENTION FROM WHAT YOU ARE DOING WITH THE OTHER HAND. PRACTICE HOW YOU ARE GOING TO MOVE YOUR HANDS IN FRONT OF THE MIRROR.

2 The magician holds up a piece of string about the length of his lower arm. He says he will lift the ice cube off the plate with the string, without tying knots or making loops.

3 He hands the string round for the spectators to check. Then he places it across the top of the ice cube.

4 The magician says some magic words and waves his arms around. Still waving with one hand, he takes a large pinch of salt with the other from under the plate.

5 He now crosses and uncrosses his hands over the plate. He passes the hand with the salt under the other hand. On one of these crossings, the magician lets the salt feed out from between his fingers onto the top of the string.

6 The magician continues to move his hands, blocking the view of the ice cube as the salt dissolves. He mutters some special made-up magic words as he does this.

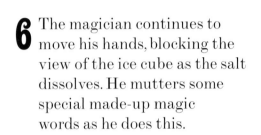

OOBA, KOOBA, ZINGLE, ZOO

7 After about 15 seconds, the magician takes hold of each end of the string. He pulls it tight and slowly lifts. The ice cube remains attached to the string as he does so.

STICKING PENCILS

1 Prior to the trick, the magician takes two new (unsharpened) wooden pencils with completely flat ends. He holds the pencils up and hands them around for the audience to check.

2 He asks for a strong volunteer to come up and hold a pencil in each hand.

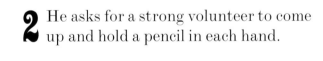

3 The magician then gets the volunteer to hold the pencils together, so that the ends are touching.

60...59...58...

...4...3...2...1

4 The magician asks the volunteer to press the pencils together as hard as he can for one minute. The magician gets the spectators to count down from 60 until the minute is up.

5 As the spectators count, the magician waves his hands slowly over the pencils.

6 When the minute is up, the magician says that he has magically locked the pencils together. He asks the volunteer to pull them apart, but it can't be done!

MAGIC FACT
THE VOLUNTEER'S MUSCLES "LOCK" AND KEEP PUSHING THE PENCILS TOGETHER, EVEN WHEN THE VOLUNTEER STOPS TRYING TO PUSH.

JUMPING COIN

1 The magician shows the audience two identical small coins.

2 He places a coin in each of his open palms. The first coin should sit exactly in the middle of his left hand. The second should sit on the bulge below his right thumb.

3 The magician shows his open palms to the audience, then flips his hands over quickly, slapping them down on the table. The coin on the right hand will shoot across to the left hand!

4 He says he has made one of the coins magically jump to his other hand. He slowly turns his right hand over. There is no coin underneath!

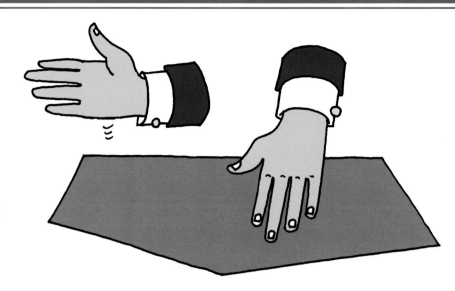

5 Now he turns his left hand over. Both coins are there!

MAGIC FACT
THE COIN IN THE MAGICIAN'S RIGHT HAND WILL "JUMP" ACROSS TO HIS LEFT HAND SO QUICKLY THAT THE AUDIENCE WILL NOT SEE IT HAPPEN.

KETCHUP CATCH-UP

ILLUSION

The magician uses his powers to levitate a packet of ketchup inside a bottle of water.

1 Prior to the trick, the magician collects several ketchup packets. He tests them, one by one, by dropping them into a bowl of water. He chooses a packet that floats, but doesn't rise right to the top.

2 Next he removes the labels from a large, empty plastic cola bottle.

25

3 The magician begins the trick by showing the packet of ketchup to the audience. Then he places it inside the plastic bottle.

4 The magician fills the bottle with water and screws on the cap.

5 He holds up the bottle so that the spectators can see the ketchup packet floating halfway down.

ONE, TWO, THREE

6 Now he tells the spectators that he will command the ketchup to sink. He waves his left hand in time with his count: "one," "two," "THREE"—and on the third count gives the bottle a slight squeeze. The ketchup sinks.

7 The magician counts again, but this time on the third count he stops squeezing. The ketchup rises again.

BALLS OF FUN

ILLUSION

The magician puts a paper ball on an upturned cup and taps lightly. He lifts the cup and the ball has gone right through it!

1 Prior to the trick, the magician finds three identical large plastic cups. He tears a paper napkin into four equal pieces, which he scrunches into balls.

2 He puts one of the paper balls into one of the cups. He stands the cup on the table so that the spectators can't see the ball inside.

3 To perform the trick, the magician tells the spectators that they will see some real magic with the simplest things—three paper balls and three plastic cups. He lines the cups up and puts a paper ball on the spectators' side of each cup. The secret fourth ball is out of sight in the middle cup.

4 Now he flips the cups over so that they're upside down. He flips the middle cup over quickly so that the ball doesn't fall out.

5 He puts one paper ball on the upturned middle cup and stacks the other two cups on top.

6 The magician says: "Now for some magic!" He taps the stack of cups lightly with his wand. He lifts up the stack of three cups and shows that the ball has gone all the way through!

7 The magician turns the cups the right way up and then dismantles the stack. The ball he placed on the upturned cup is now at the bottom of the middle cup.

8 The magician flips this cup over to cover the first ball (the one that "went through" the stack), and lines up the other two cups on either side. (Now there are two balls under the middle cup, but the audience thinks there is only one.)

9 The magician places a paper ball on the middle cup and stacks the two empty cups over it.

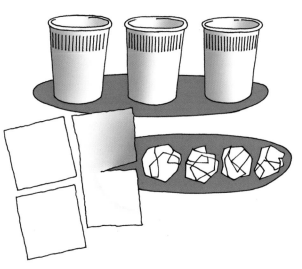

10 He taps the cups lightly twice and lifts the stack. There are now two balls underneath!

11 The magician pulls the stack apart and lines up the cups for the last time. He makes sure to cover the two paper balls with the cup that has the hidden ball. With three balls now under the middle cup (the spectators think there are two), the magician puts the last ball on the middle cup and stacks the others over it.

12 He taps the cups three times, lifts up the stack and—surprise!—all three balls are underneath!

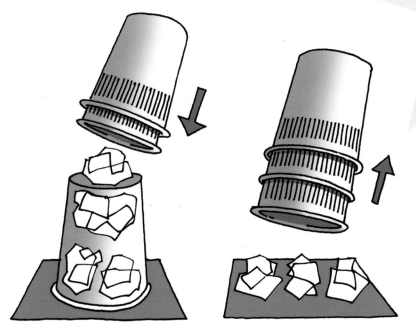

MAGIC TIP!
THIS TRICK DEPENDS ON YOUR ABILITY TO FLIP THE CUP OVER BEFORE THE BALL FALLS OUT. MAKE SURE YOU REHEARSE THAT BEFORE PERFORMING THE TRICK.

FURTHER READING

Barnhart, Norm. *Amazing Magic Tricks.*
Mankato, MN: Capstone Press, 2009.

Cassidy, John and Michael Stroud. *Klutz Book of Magic.* Palo Alto, CA: Klutz Press, 2006.

Charney, Steve. *Cool Card Tricks.* Easy Magic Tricks. Mankato, MN: Capstone Press, 2010.

Klingel, Cynthia and Robert B. Noyed. *Card Tricks.* Mankato, MN: Compass Point Books, 2002.

Longe, Bob. *The Little Giant Book of Card Tricks.* New York: Sterling Publishers Inc, 2000.

WEBSITES

For web resources related to
the subject of this book, go to:
www.windmillbooks.com/weblinks
and select this book's title.

GLOSSARY

dissolve (dih-ZOLV) To become part of a liquid when mixed with a liquid.

flourish (FLUH-rish) To wave something about in a way that makes people look at it.

grind (GRYND) To crush something into a powder.

identical (y-DEN-tih-kul) Exactly the same.

index finger (IN-deks FING-gur) The finger next to the thumb.

INDEX